Top-Notch

Tassels & Pom-Poms

Jazz up your home and accessorize your wardrobe with easy crafts ranging from a rug and pillow to purses and jewelry.

CONTENTS

LEISURE ARTS, INC.
Maumelle, Arkansas

floss-wrapped

Necklace

Shopping List

- ☐ $^{3}/_{16}$" cotton filler cord
- ☐ Embroidery floss – aqua (2 skeins), black, dark red (5 skeins), gold & lime
- ☐ Two 6mm silver cord ends with loop
- ☐ Two 5mm silver jump rings
- ☐ Silver toggle clasp
- ☐ 2" square of cardboard
- ☐ E6000® Industrial Strength Adhesive
- ☐ Two pair chain-nose jewelry pliers
- ☐ Transparent tape

1. Cut a 20" length of cotton cord; tape the cut ends. Tie the aqua floss to the cord about 1/4" from one end, leaving a 1/2" tail ***(Fig. 1)***. Holding the tail alongside the cord, wrap the aqua floss around the cord for about 3". Make sure the floss is wound firmly and no cord is showing through the floss wraps. Knot the aqua floss by passing the floss end through the last wrap and tightening. Trim the excess floss, leaving a short tail. Continue tying on and wrapping floss around the cotton cord in the following color sequence: 1" of dark red, 1/2" gold, 1/2" black, 1" lime, 1/2" black, 1/2" gold, 2" of dark red. Make sure to always hide the short tail in the wrapped sections. Wrap the remaining side to reflect the first side of necklace.
2. To make a tassel, wrap dark red floss around the cardboard about 45 times. Cut the floss along the bottom edge and remove the cardboard. Carefully place the cut floss around the center of the dark red center section of the necklace. Tightly tie a dark red piece of floss around the tassel right below the necklace; trim the excess. Refer to *Making A Tassel* (page 41, Step 2) to wrap the tassel with aqua floss. Add a dark red tassel on either side of the center tassel.
3. Trim the cotton cord ends to 1/8". Apply a drop of adhesive inside each silver cord end. Insert the cotton cord ends into the silver cord ends; let dry.
4. Use jump rings (page 44) to attach the clasp pieces to the cord ends.

Tips

For a smooth finish, wrap the floss around the cord so that the floss wraps lie side by side and do not overlap.

When wrapping, hold the floss skein loosely in one hand while turning the cord with the fingers of your other hand (as opposed to wrapping the floss skein around the cord each time).

Fig. 1

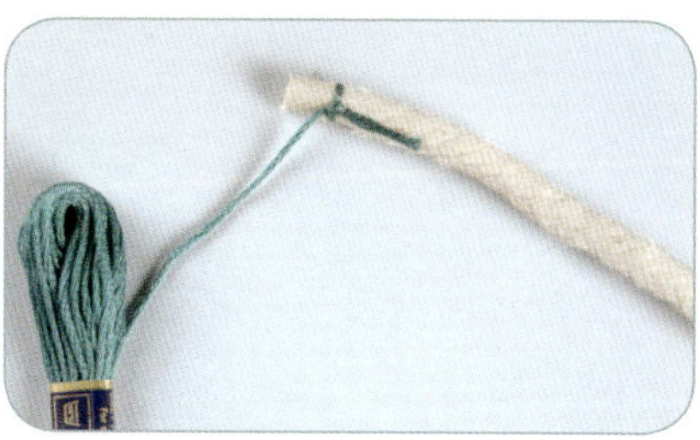

Shopping List

- ☐ 3/16" cotton filler cord
- ☐ Embroidery floss – aqua, black, dark red (2 skeins), gold & lime
- ☐ Four 6mm silver cord ends with loop
- ☐ Two 5mm silver jump rings
- ☐ Silver ear wires
- ☐ E6000® Industrial Strength Adhesive
- ☐ Two pair chain-nose jewelry pliers
- ☐ Transparent tape

floss-wrapped
Earrings

For each earring, follow Steps 1-4.

1. Cut a 4" length of cotton cord; tape the cut ends. Tie the aqua floss to the cord about 1/4" from one end, leaving a 1/2" tail ***(Fig. 1)***. Holding the tail alongside the cord, wrap the aqua floss around the cord for about 1/2". Make sure the floss is wound firmly and no cord is showing through the floss wraps. Knot the aqua floss by passing the floss end through the last wrap and tightening. Trim the excess floss, leaving a short tail. Continue tying on and wrapping floss around the cotton cord in the following color sequence: 1/4" of lime, 1/4" black, 1" gold. Make sure to always hide the short tail in the wrapped sections. Wrap the remaining side to reflect the first side of the earring.
2. To make the tassel, trim a dark red floss skein 2" from one folded end. Carefully place the cut floss around the center of the gold center section of the earring. Tightly tie a dark red piece of floss around the tassel right below the earring; trim the excess. Refer to *Making A Tassel* (page 41, Step 2) to wrap the tassel neck with aqua floss.
3. Place a silver cord end on each floss-wrapped cord end to make sure 1/4" of the aqua floss shows. Trim the cord ends if necessary. Apply a drop of adhesive inside each silver cord end. Insert each cotton cord end into a silver cord end; let dry.
4. Use a jump ring (page 44) to join the cord ends and to attach an ear wire.

Fig. 1

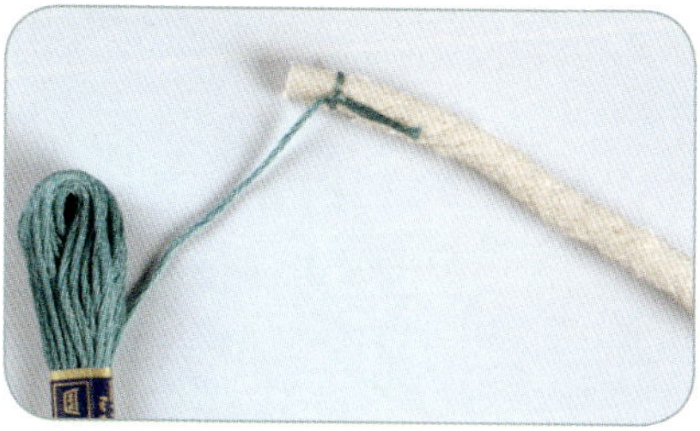

Shopping List

- ☐ Fuchsia wool felt – two 4$^{1}/_{2}$" x 6" pieces
- ☐ 28 8mm faceted purple glass beads
- ☐ Embroidery floss – light purple (7 skeins), purple (4 skeins) & dark purple (5 skeins)
- ☐ Large embroidery needle
- ☐ Wire loop beading needle
- ☐ 1$^{5}/_{8}$" pom-pom maker

mini accessory

Purse

1. Referring to **Fig. 1**, use a drinking glass or cup to draw rounded corners on the bottom corners of each felt purse piece. Cut along the drawn lines.
2. Matching the edges, pin the purse pieces together. Use 6 strands of purple floss and the embroidery needle to work *Blanket Stitches* (page 44) around the purse side and bottom edges.
3. Cut a 40" length of light purple embroidery floss. Leaving a 6"-8" tail, knot one end. Thread the opposite floss end through the beading needle. Thread the beads onto the floss, tying a knot between each bead and after the last bead.
4. Thread one floss tail of the beaded strand through the embroidery needle; securely sew the strand to one inside corner of the purse. Make sure your stitches do not show on the right side of the purse. Knot and trim the excess floss. Repeat to sew the remaining floss end to the opposite corner of the purse.
5. Follow the manufacturer's instructions to make three two-toned pom-poms (wrap one floss color on each side of pom-pom maker): two with dark purple and light purple floss and one with purple and light purple. Trim the pom-poms to about $1^1/_4$" diameter, leaving the cinching tails long.
6. Thread the cinching tails on a pom-pom onto the embroidery needle. Bring the needle from front to back on the top edge of the purse; unthread the needle. Securely tie the floss ends on the inside of the purse; trim the excess floss ends. Repeat with the remaining pom-poms.

Fig. 1

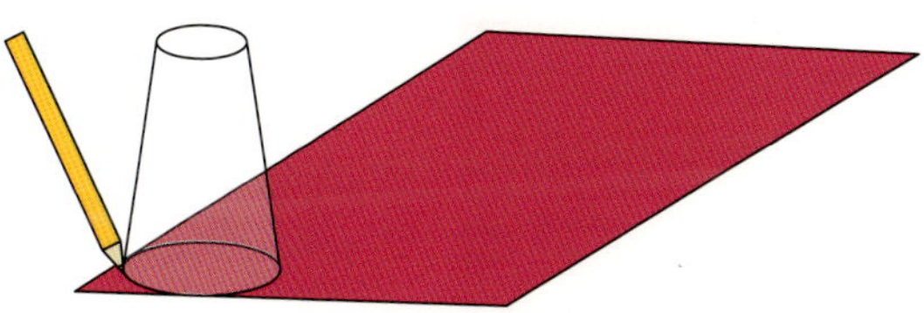

Shopping List

- ☐ 8" x 6" piece of red felt
- ☐ Embroidery floss – black, light blue (6 skeins), lime (5 skeins), red (5 skeins) & white
- ☐ Thick yarn – light blue
- ☐ Large embroidery needle
- ☐ Large plastic needle
- ☐ Polyester fiberfill
- ☐ 1 5/8" pom-pom maker
- ☐ Tracing paper
- ☐ 6" square of cardboard

heart Doorhanger

1. Cut three 36" lengths of light blue yarn. Holding all lengths together, tie an overhand knot close to one end. Braid the yarn ends for 29"; tie a temporary knot.
2. Follow *Making A Tassel* (page 41) to make a light blue floss tassel, wrapping the floss around the cardboard about 25 times and wrapping the tassel neck with red and black floss.
3. Follow the manufacturer's instructions to make a lime green floss pom-pom, a red floss pom-pom, and a light blue floss pom-pom. Trim the pom-poms to about 1 1/2" diameter.
4. Fold one end of the braid into a 4" long loop. Secure the loop by wrapping with light blue floss and finishing just like you did the tassel neck. Tie an overhand knot about 1" from the wrapped area. Thread the braid onto the plastic needle and slide the lime green pom-pom onto the yarn braid (be sure the pom-pom is centered). Tie a knot close to the pom-pom. Tie another knot about 1" from the last knot. Slide the red pom-pom onto the yarn braid and tie a knot. Tie another knot about 1" from the last knot. Slide the light blue pom-pom onto the yarn braid and tie a knot. Tie another knot about 1" from the last knot; tie a tight knot to secure the braid about 1 1/2" below the very last knot. Trim away any excess braid.
5. Trace the heart pattern (page 47) onto tracing paper; cut out. Use the pattern to cut 2 felt heart pieces. Using six strands of white floss, work seven *French knots* (page 45) on one heart piece. Thread the tassel floss ends through the embroidery needle. Sew the tassel to the wrong side of the remaining heart piece near the bottom point, making sure the stitches do not show on the right side. Matching the outer edges, place the heart pieces together. Starting near the heart top center point, work black *Blanket Stitches* around the outer edges, stopping just before you reach the starting point. Slip a small amount of fiberfill into the heart; slip the knotted end of the yarn braid into the heart. Continue working Blanket Stitches to close the opening.

Shopping List

- ☐ 8" x 4" piece of aqua felt
- ☐ Embroidery floss – aqua, dark blue & white
- ☐ Thick yarn – dark blue, light blue & mint green
- ☐ Large embroidery needle
- ☐ Large plastic needle
- ☐ Polyester fiberfill
- ☐ $2^{1}/_{2}$" pom-pom maker
- ☐ Tracing paper
- ☐ 6" square of cardboard

moon Doorhanger

1. Cut three 36" lengths of light blue yarn. Holding all lengths together, tie an overhand knot close to one end. Braid the yarn ends for 29"; tie a knot. Thread the yarn ends through the plastic needle and set aside.
2. Follow *Making A Tassel* (page 41) to make a tassel, wrapping the dark blue, light blue, and mint green yarns around the cardboard 3-4 times each and wrapping the aqua floss around the cardboard 5-6 times. Wrap the tassel neck with aqua floss.
3. Follow the manufacturer's instructions to make a dark blue yarn pom-pom and a mint green yarn pom-pom. Trim the pom-poms to about 2" diameter.
4. Trace the moon pattern (page 47) onto tracing paper; cut out. Use the pattern to cut 2 felt moon pieces. Using six strands of white floss work five *French knots* (page 45) on one moon piece. Matching the outer edges, place the moon pieces together and work dark blue *Blanket Stitches* around the outer edges; just before you finish stitching, slip a small amount of fiberfill into the moon.
5. Thread the yarn braid up through the tassel center; pull until tight. Tie an overhand knot about 1" above the tassel. Slide the mint green pom-pom onto the yarn braid (be sure the pom-pom is centered). Tie a knot close to the pom-pom. Tie another knot about 1" from the pom-pom. Slide the dark blue pom-pom onto the yarn braid and tie a knot. Tie another knot about 1" from the pom-pom.
6. Thread the yarn braid through the moon bottom and out through the moon top. Fold the braid into a loop and tuck the loose ends into the moon. Using aqua floss, hand sew several small stitches to secure the braided loop.

Shopping List

- ☐ Fabric – two 8" x 10" pieces of 5-6 fabrics
- ☐ Medium weight black yarn
- ☐ Embroidery floss – red (8 skeins) & black (6 skeins)
- ☐ 6mm white rope – about 3-4 yards
- ☐ Two 6mm silver cord ends with loops
- ☐ Two 10mm silver jump rings
- ☐ Paper-backed fusible web
- ☐ Pinking shears
- ☐ Two pair chain-nose jewelry pliers
- ☐ $1^5/_8$" pom-pom maker
- ☐ Large embroidery needle
- ☐ E6000® Industrial Strength Adhesive
- ☐ Tracing paper
- ☐ Liquid fray preventative
- ☐ Transparent tape
- ☐ Large safety pin
- ☐ 4" x 6"piece of cardboard

pennant Banner

1. Follow the manufacturer's instructions to fuse two matching fabric pieces wrong sides together. Trace the pennant pattern (page 46) onto tracing paper and cut out. Use the pattern and pinking shears to cut a total of 7 pennants. Apply the fray preventative to the cut edges of each pennant.
2. Press the top edge of each pennant $^1/_2$" to the wrong side. Sew approximately $^3/_8$" from the folded edge, creating a casing for the rope.
3. Make three black and four red 3" long tassels (page 41), wrapping each tassel about 50 times. Thread the long floss tails on a tassel onto the embroidery needle. Bring the needle from the front to the back on a pennant tip; unthread the needle. Tie the floss ends on the pennant wrong side. Trim the floss ends. Repeat to attach a tassel to each pennant.
4. Wrap tape around each end of the white rope. Attach a large safety pin to one end. Use the safety pin to thread the cord through the pennants, alternating the colors as desired.
5. Follow the manufacturer's instructions to make six black yarn pom-poms; trim the pom-poms to about 1$^1/_2$" diameter, leaving the cinching tails long. Use the cinching tails to tie the pom-poms to the rope, placing the pom-poms between the pennants. Trim the excess yarn.
6. Adhere the silver cord ends to the ends of the rope; allow to dry.
7. For the tassels on the rope ends, make two 5" long tassels, wrapping about 45 times with red floss and 15 times with black floss; tie the tassel necks with black floss. Open a jump ring (page 44); slip the jump ring through the top of a tassel and the loop on a cord end. Close the jump ring. Repeat with the remaining jump ring and tassel.

tassel
Key Chain

Shopping List

- ☐ Swivel clip
- ☐ 25mm split ring
- ☐ Embroidery floss – aqua, coral (2 skeins), fuchsia, & gold
- ☐ Two 8mm x 6mm green wooden beads
- ☐ 5mm silver spacer bead
- ☐ 20-gauge wire
- ☐ Large embroidery needle
- ☐ Jewelry pliers – round-nose & chain-nose
- ☐ Wire cutters

Double Pom-pom Key Chain instructions on page 16.

1. Remove the labels from the skeins of coral floss; lay them side by side. Tie the gold floss to the coral floss bundle about 2" from the top, leaving a 1/2" tail ***(Fig. 1)***. Holding the tail alongside the bundle, wrap the gold floss around the coral floss bundle for about 5/8". Knot the gold floss and trim the excess, leaving a short tail. Continue tying on and wrapping floss around the coral bundle, in the following color sequence: fuchsia (3/8"), gold (3/8"), fuchsia (3/8"), gold (5/8"). Make sure to always hide the short tail in the wrapped sections.
2. Gently fold the wrapped bundle into a loop. Wrap the bundle with aqua floss in the same manner as you wrapped before, but leave a long tail after the last knot. Thread the floss tail onto the embroidery needle. Slip the needle under the wrapped area and pull out through the top. Go back down through the center of the tassel, remove the needle, and trim the floss, hiding the end in the coral floss. Trim the coral tassel as desired.
3. Cut a 4" wire length. Make a large wrapped loop (page 43, ignoring the bead references) slipping the floss wrapped top of the tassel into the wire loop before wrapping it. Slide on a wooden bead, the spacer bead, and the remaining wooden bead. Make a wrapped loop, slipping the split ring into the loop before wrapping it.
4. Attach the split ring to the swivel clip.

Fig. 1

double pom-pom Key Chain

Photo on page 14.

Shopping List

- ☐ Swivel clip
- ☐ 25mm split ring
- ☐ Thick yarn – light blue & hot pink
- ☐ Embroidery floss – light blue & fuchsia
- ☐ 10mm blue bead
- ☐ 1⁵⁄₈" pom-pom maker
- ☐ Large embroidery needle
- ☐ Liquid fray preventative
- ☐ 3" square of cardboard

1. Follow the manufacturer's instructions to make a light blue yarn pom-pom; trim the pom-pom to about 1³⁄₈" diameter. Make a light blue and hot pink yarn pom-pom; trim the pom-pom to about 1³⁄₈" diameter.
2. Make a 2" fuchsia floss tassel (page 41), wrapping the tassel about 32 times and tying the tassel neck with light blue floss. Trim the ends as desired.
3. Thread the long floss tails on the tassel onto the embroidery needle. Thread the needle through the bead, the center of the blue pom-pom, and the center of the two-tone pom-pom. Tie the floss ends to the split ring with a few knots. Apply a drop of fray preventative to the knots; allow to dry. Trim the floss ends.
4. Attach the split ring to the swivel clip.

black mini
Purse

Shopping List

- ☐ Black felt – 6" x 13" piece
- ☐ Scrap of fuchsia felt
- ☐ 30" length of thick black & white yarn
- ☐ Thick black yarn for pom-pom
- ☐ Embroidery floss – black, fuchsia (4 skeins) & mauve
- ☐ Large embroidery needle
- ☐ Sew-on snap
- ☐ 3" x 6" piece of cardboard
- ☐ 1" pom-pom maker
- ☐ Tracing paper

1. Trace the heart pattern (page 19) onto tracing paper and cut out. Use the pattern to cut out a fuchsia felt heart.
2. From the black felt, cut a 4$^1/_2$" x 5" piece and a 5" x 7$^1/_2$" piece. Center the heart on one short end of the larger felt piece with the heart point on the felt edge. Draw a line on the black felt that "cuts" the heart in half (do not mark the heart piece). Draw around the lower half of the heart. Remove the fuchsia heart and cut out purse edge along the drawn lines, rounding the corners ***(Fig. 1)***.
3. Referring to **Fig. 2**, cut a window in the cardboard piece.

Fig. 1

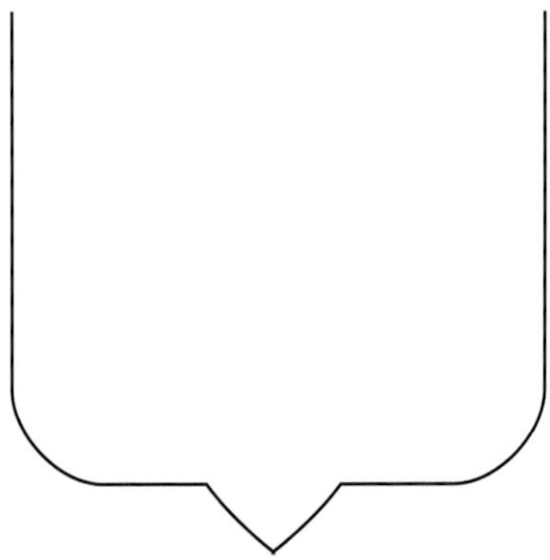

Fig. 2

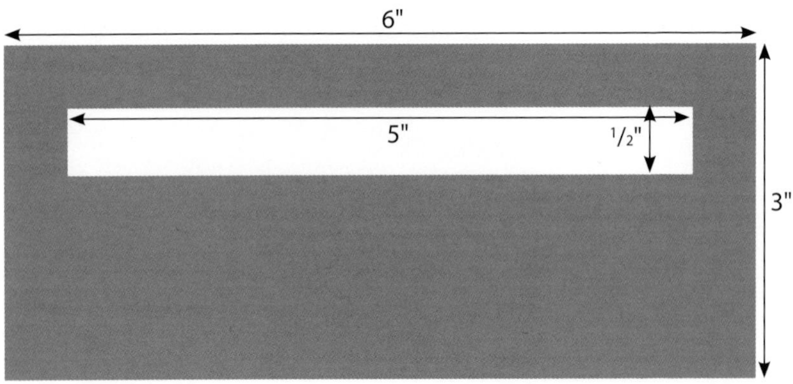

4. To make the purse fringe, start at the bottom left and wrap a single, solid layer of fuchsia floss (use 3 skeins) around the cardboard piece. Again starting at the bottom left, randomly wrap mauve floss around the cardboard piece. Sew a tight zigzag stitch over the floss in the open window area of the cardboard.
5. Cut the fringe along the top and bottom cardboard edges. Remove the cardboard piece.
6. Matching the 5" long edges, stack the large felt piece, the fringe, and the smaller felt piece; make sure the zigzag stitching on the fringe is covered by the smaller felt piece. Zigzag stitch around the side and bottom edges of the felt, being sure to catch the fringe in the stitching. Trim the fringe as desired.
7. Pin the heart to the right side of the purse flap, matching the edges. Use six strands of fuchsia embroidery floss to work *Blanket Stitches* (page 44) around the heart, attaching it to the flap. Work Blanket Stitches along the curved edges of the flap.
8. Follow the manufacturer's instructions to make a black yarn pom-pom. Trim the pom-pom to about 3/4", leaving the cinching tails long.
9. Thread the cinching tails on the pom-pom onto the embroidery needle. Bring the needle from front to back on the heart on the purse flap; unthread the needle. Tie the yarn ends with a tight knot on the wrong side; trim the excess yarn ends.
10. Use black floss to sew the snap to the flap and purse front. For the purse handle, knot the ends of the black and white yarn together. Lay the handle across the wrong side of the flap right above the purse front. Slipstitch the handle to the flap.

Shopping List

- ☐ 34 8mm cream beads
- ☐ 66 3mm x 5mm black glass rondelle beads
- ☐ 18 5mm silver spacer beads
- ☐ 6 6/0 black seed beads
- ☐ Medium weight black yarn
- ☐ Embroidery floss – black (3 skeins) & ecru
- ☐ Large embroidery needle
- ☐ 1" pom-pom maker
- ☐ Craft glue
- ☐ 4" square of cardboard

Tassel Earrings instructions on page 22.

pom-pom & tassel Necklace

1. Follow the manufacturer's instructions to make seven black yarn pom-poms. Trim the pom-poms to about $^{3}/_{4}$" diameter.
2. Follow *Making A Tassel* (page 41) to make a black and ecru floss tassel, wrapping each color 7-10 times around the cardboard before switching colors. Switch back and forth until you have wrapped with each floss color 3-4 times. Wrap the tassel neck with ecru floss.
3. Cut a 45" length of black floss and fold in half. Tie a double knot at the folded end, a few inches from the end. Thread the free floss ends onto the needle. Pass the needle through the tassel center and out through the tassel loop. Pull the floss tight. Thread one pom-pom onto the floss (be sure the pom-pom is centered) and tie a tight knot close to the pom-pom.
4. Apply glue to the free floss ends, keeping them separate; allow to dry. Trim the dried glue ends at an angle to create a sharp point that can be threaded through the beads
5. Thread the beads and pom-poms on each floss end in the following sequence:
   - 2 cream beads, 1 silver spacer bead, 1 black bead, 3 cream beads,1 silver spacer bead, and 1 pom-pom (thread floss onto embroidery needle first)
   - 1 silver spacer bead, 3 cream beads, 1 silver spacer bead, 1 black bead, 3 cream beads, 1 silver spacer bead, and 1 pom-pom (thread floss onto embroidery needle first)
   - 1 silver spacer bead, 3 cream beads, 1 silver spacer bead, 1 black bead, 1 cream bead, 1 silver spacer bead, 1 pom-pom (thread floss onto embroidery needle first), 1 silver spacer bead, and 2 cream beads
   - 30 black beads

   Tie a knot close to the last bead.
6. Knot the floss ends together with a knot close to the last beads. Add three seed beads to each floss end; knot each end and trim excess floss.

tassel

Earrings

Photo on page 20.

Shopping List

- ☐ Two 8mm cream beads
- ☐ Two 5mm silver spacer beads
- ☐ Two 3mm x 5mm black glass rondelle beads
- ☐ Two 10mm silver jump rings
- ☐ Two silver ear wires
- ☐ Two silver eye pins
- ☐ Embroidery floss – black (3 skeins) & ecru
- ☐ Jewelry pliers – chain-nose & round-nose
- ☐ Wire cutters
- ☐ 4" square of cardboard

For each earring, follow Steps 1-4.

1. To make the bead connector, thread a cream bead, silver spacer bead and a black bead on an eye pin. Make a loop (page 42) on the wire end.
2. Follow *Making A Tassel* (page 41) to make a black and ecru floss tassel, wrapping each color 7-10 times around the cardboard before switching colors. Switch back and forth until you have wrapped with each floss color 3-4 times. Wrap the tassel neck with ecru floss.
3. Open a jump ring (page 44); slip the jump ring through the top of a tassel and the bottom loop on the bead connector. Close the jump ring.
4. Attach an ear wire.

denim
Bag

Shopping List

- ☐ Old jeans pant leg about 12" long
- ☐ 2 1/2 yards navy blue satin cord
- ☐ Embroidery floss – dark blue (10 skeins) & light blue (9 skeins)
- ☐ Assorted iron-on patches
- ☐ Safety pin
- ☐ Transparent tape
- ☐ Crochet hook

1. Turn the jeans pant leg inside out and use a 1/2" seam allowance to sew across the bottom, curving the seam at the corners to create a rounded bottom. Trim away the excess bulk.
2. Press the pant leg top 1/2" to the wrong side; press 2" to the wrong side again. To create the casing for the drawstring cord, topstitch 1" from top edge of bag. Topstitch 5/8" below the first line of stitching. Turn the bag right side out.
3. Arrange the patches on the bag front, keeping the patches below the casing. Follow the manufacturer's instructions to adhere the patches to the bag.
4. Carefully cut a small slit on either side of bag front and back, being sure to cut near the side seams, within the casing area, and only through the top layer of denim ***(Fig. 1)***.

Fig. 1

5. Cut two 45" cord lengths; wrap the ends with transparent tape. Attach the safety pin to one cord end. Slide the safety pin into one casing hole on the bag front and bring it out the opposite casing hole on the bag front. Securely join the cord ends to each other with machine zigzag stitches. Repeat with the remaining cord on the bag back. Slide the joined area of each cord into its casing so that it is hidden.
6. Carefully cut 19 slits along the bottom edge of the bag, starting $^1/_2$" from one end and $^1/_2$" from the bottom and spacing slits about $^1/_4$" apart ***(Fig. 2)***. Be sure to cut through all denim layers.
7. To add the fringe, remove the labels from a dark blue floss skein; do not unwind the skein. Trim off one folded end. Use the crochet hook to pull the remaining folded skein end through the first slit, pulling the floss from the back to the front; pull the cut floss ends through the loop ***(Fig. 3)***. Pull the floss ends to tighten the knot. Repeat to add the remaining fringe, alternating floss colors. Trim the floss ends evenly.

Fig. 2

Fig. 3

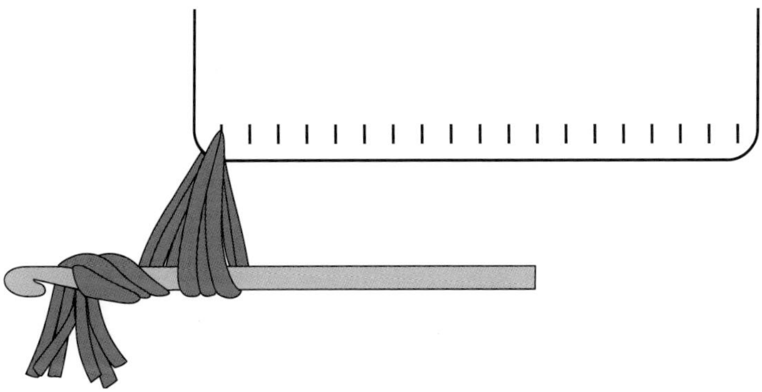

Chandelier

Shopping List

- ☐ 9" wood embroidery hoop
- ☐ Embroidery floss – mauve (5 skeins), mint green (13 skeins) & white (8 skeins)
- ☐ Medium weight yarn – apricot & mint green
- ☐ 30 10mm faceted translucent pink beads
- ☐ 2 1/2" pom-pom maker
- ☐ Large embroidery needle
- ☐ Hot glue gun & glue sticks
- ☐ Liquid fray preventative

1. To make a tassel, cut a 10" length from a floss skein. Slip the 10" length through the loop on one end of the floss skein and tie a knot. Wrap the tassel neck with contrasting floss (page 41, Step 2). Remove the labels from the floss and trim to 4" long. Place a drop of fray preventative on the knots; let dry. Make 3 white tassels tied with mauve floss, 3 white tassels tied with mint green floss, 3 mint green tassels tied with mauve floss, and 3 mauve tassels tied with mint green floss.
2. Follow the manufacturer's instructions to make 3 mint green and 3 apricot yarn pom-poms. Trim the pom-poms to about 1 3/4" diameter.
3. To make a white/mauve beaded tassel, cut an 18" length of white floss and thread onto the needle. Tie a double knot at one end. Slip the needle through the bottom of a white/mauve tassel and bring the needle out through the tassel head. Knot the floss about 1" from the tassel top. Slide a bead onto the floss and knot the floss right next to the bead. Repeat to add 2 more beads. Repeat to make two more white/mauve beaded tassels. Set the beaded tassels aside.

4. To make a mauve/mint green beaded tassel, cut an 18" length of mauve floss and thread onto the needle. Tie a double knot at one end. Slip the needle through the bottom of a mauve/mint green tassel and bring the needle out through the tassel top. Knot the floss about 1" from the tassel head. Slide a bead onto the floss and knot the floss right next to the bead. Repeat to add 1 more bead. Repeat to make two more mauve/mint green beaded tassels. Set the beaded tassels aside.
5. To make a mint green/mauve plain tassel, cut an 18" length of mint green floss and thread onto the needle. Tie a double knot at one end. Slip the needle through the bottom of a mint green/mauve tassel and bring the needle out through the tassel top. Repeat to make two more mint green/mauve plain tassels. Set the plain tassels aside.
6. To make a white/mint green plain tassel, cut an 18" length of white floss and thread onto the needle. Tie a double knot at one end. Slip the needle through the bottom of a white/mint green tassel and bring the needle out through the tassel top. Repeat to make two more white/mint green plain tassels. Set the plain tassels aside.
7. To make mint green plain pom-pom, cut an 18" length of mint green floss and thread onto the needle. Tie a double knot at one end. Slip the needle through the center of a mint green pom-pom. Repeat to make two more mint green plain pom-poms. Set the plain pom-poms aside.
8. To make an apricot beaded pom-pom, cut an 18" length of mauve floss and thread onto the needle. Tie a double knot at one end. Slip the needle through the center of an apricot pom-pom. Knot the floss about 1 1/2" from the pom-pom. Slide a bead onto the floss and knot the floss right next to the bead. Repeat to add 4 more beads, leaving 1" between the beads. Repeat to make three more apricot beaded pom-poms. Set the beaded pom-poms aside.

9. Cut three 36" lengths of mint green floss; matching the ends, fold the floss lengths in half and tie a knot near the folded end. Dividing the floss into 3 groups of 2 strands each, braid the floss until you are about 2" from the end; knot loosely to hold the braid in place. Repeat to make 4 braided floss lengths.
10. Untie the loose knots on the braided strands. Matching the ends and keeping the braids the same length, knot the braided strands together. Trim the floss ends evenly.
11. Wrap the loose end of one braided strand around the hoop a few times and neatly hot glue in place. Repeat to glue another braided strand to the opposite side of the hoop. Hot glue the remaining braided strands equidistant from the glued-on strands.
12. It is easier to add the dangles (tassels and pom-poms made in Steps 3-8) if the hoop is hanging. Four dangles will fit between each braided strand. Tie each dangle to the hoop with a temporary knot, placing the dangles as desired.
13. Adjust the tassel and pom-poms so that all strands are different lengths. Once placement is final, untie each knot and wrap the floss ends around the hoop a few times, neatly hot gluing as necessary. Trim any excess floss.
14. Wrap the entire hoop with mint green floss, covering the floss ends and hot gluing in place as necessary.

lariat Necklace

Shopping List

- ☐ 48" length of 3/16" brown suede cord (flat lace)
- ☐ Two 5mm silver beads
- ☐ Two silver crimp-style cord ends
- ☐ Two 10mm silver jump rings
- ☐ Two silver eye pins
- ☐ Embroidery floss – dark aqua (3 skeins)
- ☐ Jewelry pliers - chain-nose & round-nose
- ☐ Wire cutters
- ☐ Craft glue

1. Lay one suede cord end in one crimp-style cord end, apply a drop of glue, and use the chain-nose pliers to fold the tabs over the suede end ***(Fig. 1)***. Repeat with the opposite end of the suede cord.
2. To make the bead connector, thread a bead on an eye pin. Make a loop (page 42) on the wire end. Repeat with the remaining eye pin and bead.
3. To make each tassel, cut a 10" length of floss. Slip the 10" length through the loop on one end of another skein of floss and tie a temporary knot. Wrap the tassel neck (page 41, Step 2). Remove the labels from the floss and trim to 5" long.
4. Open a jump ring (page 44); slip the jump ring through the tassel loop and the bottom loop on a bead connector. Close the jump ring. Remove the temporary knot from the tassel loop. Open the remaining loop on the beaded connector and slip it through a cord end. Repeat with the remaining tassel, jump ring, and bead connector on the opposite end of the suede cord.

Fig. 1

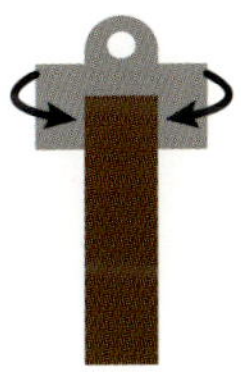

Flower Pot

Shopping List

- ☐ 4" diameter clay flower pot
- ☐ 3 3/4" diameter foam ball
- ☐ Embroidery floss – fuchsia, lavender, pink & purple (14-20 skeins total)
- ☐ 11-14 3/4" diameter two-hole buttons – mix of pink & purple
- ☐ Pom-pom makers – 1 3/8" & 1 5/8"
- ☐ Acrylic paint – black, violet & white
- ☐ 1/2" paint brush
- ☐ Clear acrylic spray sealer
- ☐ Hand sewing needle
- ☐ Long straight pins

1. Paint flower pot base violet; paint rim white. Allow to dry. Add white dots to painted base and black stripes to painted rim; allow to dry. Spray pot with sealer; allow to dry.
2. Cut the foam ball in half. Gently push the ball into the flower pot until it is secure and does not move.
3. Follow the manufacturer's instructions to make 11-14 pom-poms, mixing up the colors and sizes (use 2 floss skeins to make the larger pom-poms). Flatten each pom-pom and trim as desired. Use floss to sew a button to each pom-pom center.
4. Arrange the pom-pom flowers on the foam ball. Secure each flower to the foam with a straight pin, hiding the pin under the button.

Pillow

Shopping List

- ☐ 14" square pillow insert
- ☐ Four 8" fabric squares for pillow front
- ☐ 15" square of fabric for pillow back
- ☐ Polyester fiberfill
- ☐ Buttons – 1 5/8" diameter flower-shaped for front & 1/2" diameter for back
- ☐ Embroidery floss for each tassel: 2 medium tone skeins, 1 light tone skein & 1 contrasting skein
- ☐ Long straight needle
- ☐ 6" square of cardboard
- ☐ Liquid fray preventative

Always match the right sides and raw edges and use a 1/2" seam allowance when sewing.

1. For the pillow front, sew the squares together to form a 15" square. Press the seam allowances open.
2. Mark the center of the 15" fabric square. Leaving an opening for turning, sew the pillow front and back together. Trim the corners, turn right side out, and press.
3. Follow *Making A Tassel* (page 41) to wrap the cardboard with 2 medium tone and 1 light tone floss skeins; use the contrasting floss skein to complete the tassel. Make 4 tassels in desired colors.
4. Thread the long floss tails of a tassel through the needle; insert the needle into one corner of the pillow. Remove the needle. Securely knot the floss ends inside the pillow and trim. Add a drop of fray preventative to the floss ends. Repeat to add a tassel to each corner of the pillow.
5. Place a small amount of fiberfill into each corner of the pillow. Place the pillow insert into the pillow. Slipstitch the pillow opening closed.
6. To tuft the pillow, use a 24" floss length to sew the flower button to the center front and the round button to the center back at the dot. Pull the floss tightly to tuft the pillow. Sew through the buttons several times; securely knot the floss and trim the excess.

Throw

Shopping List

- ☐ $1^7/_8$ yards of fleece fabric (we used grey) or a ready-made throw
- ☐ Chunky yarn in two colors (we used black & cream)
- ☐ Large embroidery needle
- ☐ Pom-pom makers – $2^1/_2$" & $1^5/_8$"
- ☐ Liquid fray preventative

1. If you are making the throw, trim the fleece fabric to 53" x 66". Machine zigzag stitch close to the cut edges to give them some stability. Skip this step if you have a ready-made throw.
2. Use the pom-pom makers to make 11 large cream pom-poms, 12 small black pom-poms, and 11 large mixed color pom-poms. Trim the pom-poms to about 2" and $1^1/_2$" diameter, leaving the cinching tails long.
3. Thread the cinching tails of a black pom-pom through the needle; thread the needle through one corner of the fleece. Remove the needle. Securely knot the yarn ends and trim. Add a drop of fray preventative to the yarn ends. Repeat to add a black pom-pom to each corner of the throw.
4. Attach the remaining pom-poms to the throw, spacing them about 6" apart along all four throw edges and alternating colors.

pom-pom

Rug

Shopping List

- ☐ Three coordinating thick yarn colors (we used 135 yards of cream, 160 yards of black & 178 yards of black/cream striped yarn)
- ☐ 14" x 28" non-skid rug pad
- ☐ Crochet hook (optional)

1. *Refer to Photos 1-4 when make finger pom-poms.* To make each pom-pom, set aside a 12" yarn length. Pulling the yarn directly from the skein and holding the end with your thumb, wrap the yarn around your fingers about 50-55 times. Pull the pom-pom off your fingers. Tightly knot the 12" yarn length around the middle of the wrapped area and cut the looped ends. Make a total of 50 pom-poms (we made 15 cream, 15 black, and 20 black/white striped yarn pom-poms.

Photo 1

Photo 2

Photo 3

Photo 4

2. Arrange the pom-poms in the striped pattern on the rug pad. Make sure they are spaced so that the rug pad does not show.
3. Beginning at one corner about 1" in on both sides, pull the yarn tails through the rug pad through two adjacent holes. Tie a single knot on the wrong side of the pad (you'll go back and double knot the pom-poms once you are happy with the placement). It may be helpful to use a crochet hook to pull the yarn tail through the pad. Continue adding pom-poms for this first row, making sure you use holes in the same row of the rug pad grid to keep the row straight. Continue adding pom-poms in this manner until all are on the rug pad.
4. Check the rug from the front to be sure you are happy with the pom-pom placement; adjust any pom-poms as needed. On the wrong side, tie all yarn tails in double knots and trim the excess yarn.
5. For the fringe, cut 72 12" black yarn lengths. On one short end of the rug, skip the end hole and snip the rug pad grid between 2 holes to make a larger hole. Skip the next hole and snip the grid away again. Continue skipping and snipping across the rug end. Repeat on the opposite end. Holding two yarn lengths together, fold them in half and attach them to the rug through the snipped holes with a Lark's Head Knot ***(Fig. 1)***, threading from front to back through the hole and pulling the yarn ends through the loop. Tighten the knot. Continue to add fringe on both rug ends. Trim fringe as desired.

Fig. 1

general

Instructions

Making A Tassel

1. Wrap yarn or floss around the cardboard the specified number of times. Trim the yarn or floss from the skein. Slip a 16" length of yarn or floss behind the wraps and bring it to the top of the cardboard; tie a secure knot. Cut the yarn or floss loops on the end opposite the knot ***(Fig. 1)***. Remove the cardboard.

Fig. 1

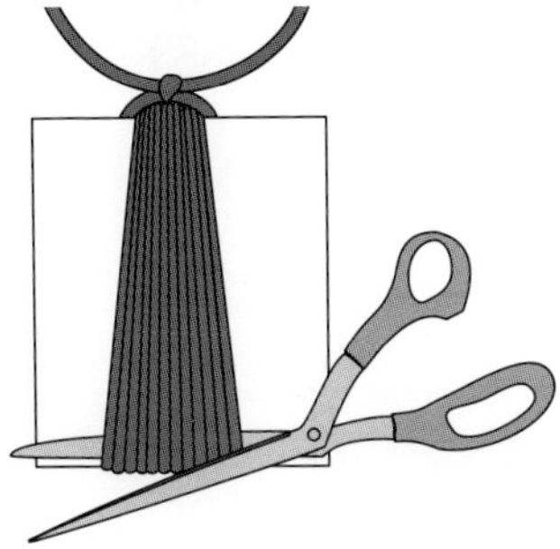

2. Form a loop with a 12" yarn or floss length. Wrap the yarn or floss around the tassel neck about $^{1}/_{2}$" below the knot ***(Fig. 2)***. Bring the end through the loop ***(Fig. 3)***. Pull firmly on the opposite end until the yarn or floss end disappears.

Fig. 2

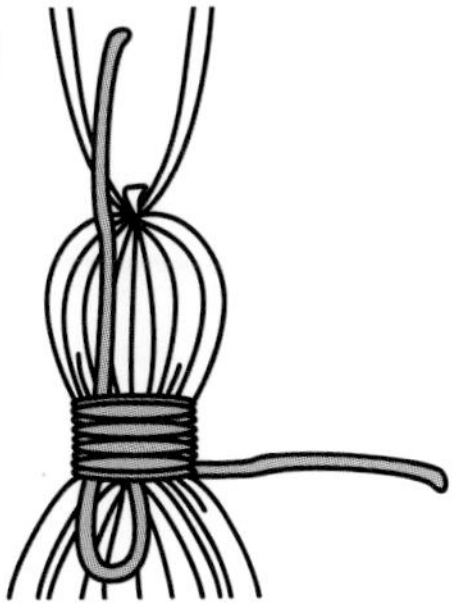

Fig. 3

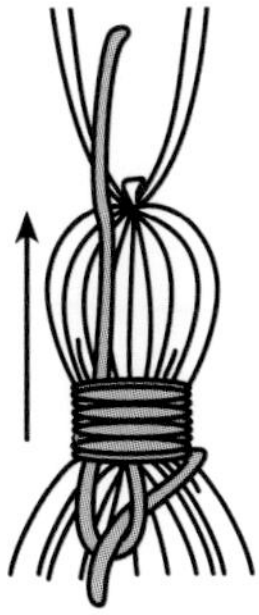

3. Trim the yarn or floss ends and place a drop of glue or liquid fray preventative on each end.

Making A Loop on a Head Pin or Eye Pin

1. Slide your bead(s) on a head pin or eye pin. Leaving about 1/2", cut off the excess wire. If you are making a larger loop, leave more wire at the end.
2. Using the chain-nose pliers, bend the wire at a 90° angle ***(Fig. 4)***. Grasp the wire end with the round-nose pliers. Turn the pliers and bend the wire into a loop ***(Figs. 5-6)***. Release the pliers. Straighten or twist the loop further if necessary.

Fig. 4

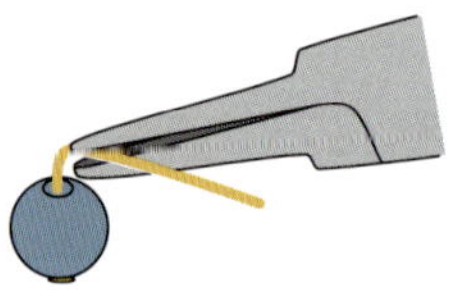

Fig. 5

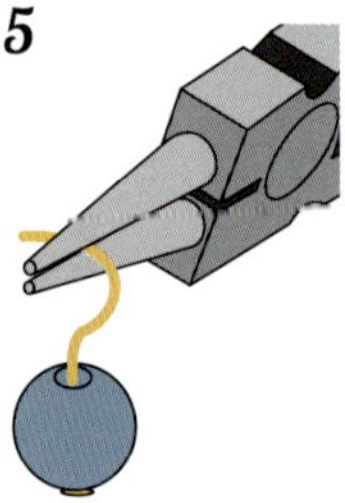

Fig. 6

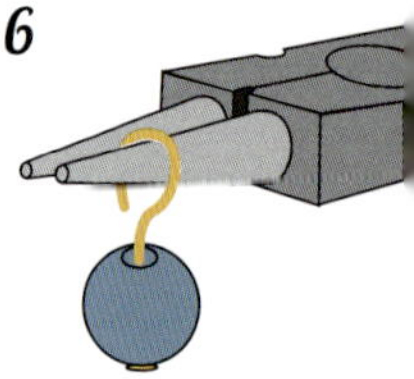

Making A Wrapped Loop on a Head Pin, Eye Pin, or Wire End

1. Slide your bead(s) on a head pin, eye pin, or wire end. Using the chain-nose pliers, bend the wire at a 90° angle about 1/8" above the bead *(Fig. 7)*.

2. Grasp the wire with the round-nose pliers at the 90° bend. Use your fingers to push the wire around the barrel of the pliers ***(Fig. 8)***. Remove the pliers.

Fig. 7

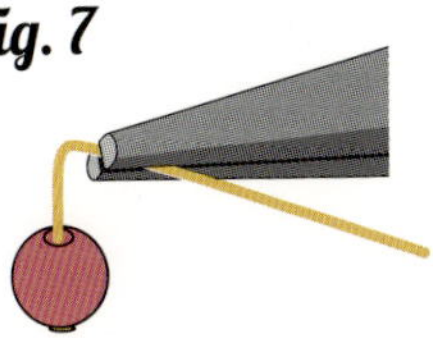

Fig. 8

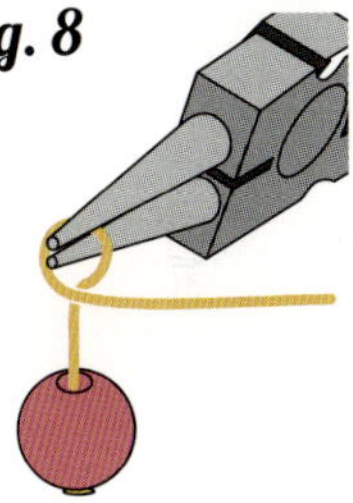

3. Now is the time to slide the loop onto your project or to add something to the wrapped loop. Holding the loop with the chain-nose pliers, use a second pair of chain-nose pliers to wrap the wire end around itself above the bead 3-5 times ***(Fig. 9)***. Trim the excess wire and tuck the wire end into the wraps with chain-nose pliers.

Fig. 9

Opening and Closing a Jump Ring

Pick up a jump ring with a pair of chain-nose pliers. With a second pair of chain-nose pliers, gently hold the other side of the ring. Open the ring by pulling one pair of pliers toward you while pushing the other away ***(Fig. 10)***. Close the ring by pushing and pulling the pliers in opposite directions, bringing the ring ends back together. Open and close loops on head pins or eye pins the same way.

Fig. 10

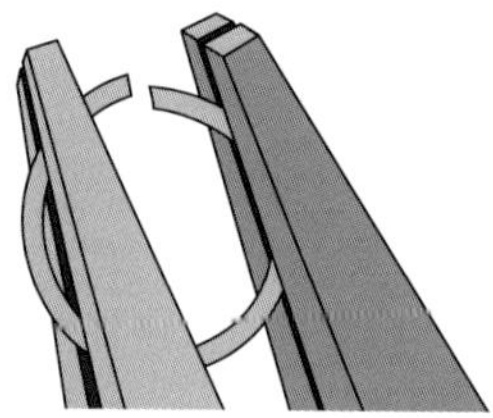

Embroidery Stitches

*When stitching, always come **up** at **1** and all **odd** numbers and go **down** at **2** and all **even** numbers.*

Blanket Stitch

Referring to **Fig. 11**, bring the needle up at 1. Keeping the floss below the point of the needle, go down at 2 and come up at 3. Continue working as shown in **Fig. 12**.

Fig. 11

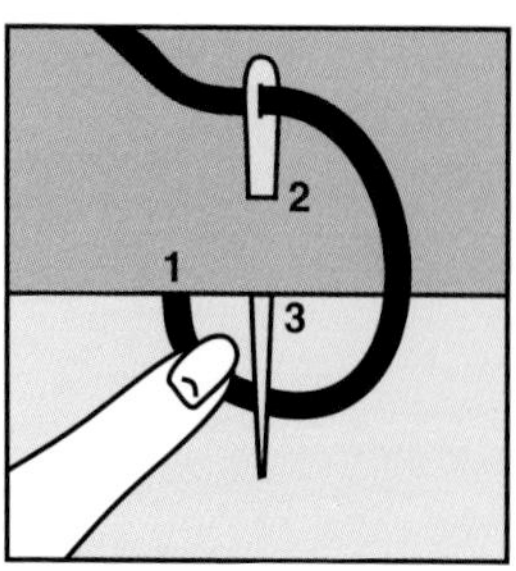

Fig. 12

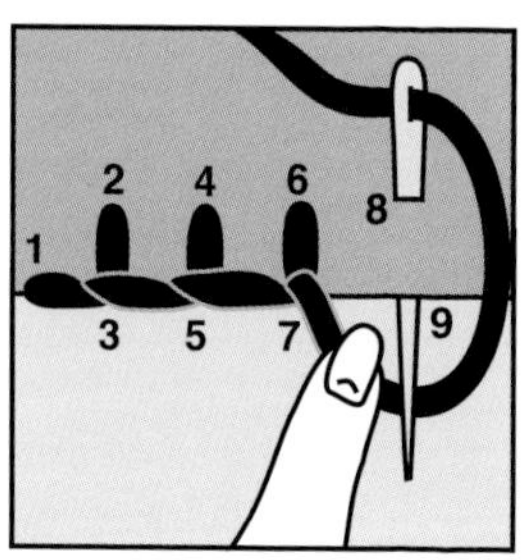

French Knot

Referring to **Fig. 13**, bring the needle up at 1. Wrap the floss once around the needle and insert the needle at 2, holding the floss with non-stitching fingers. Tighten the knot and pull the needle through the fabric, holding the floss until it must be released. For larger knots, use more floss strands; wrap only once.

Fig. 13

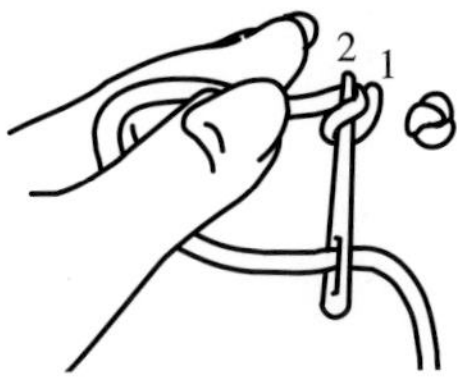

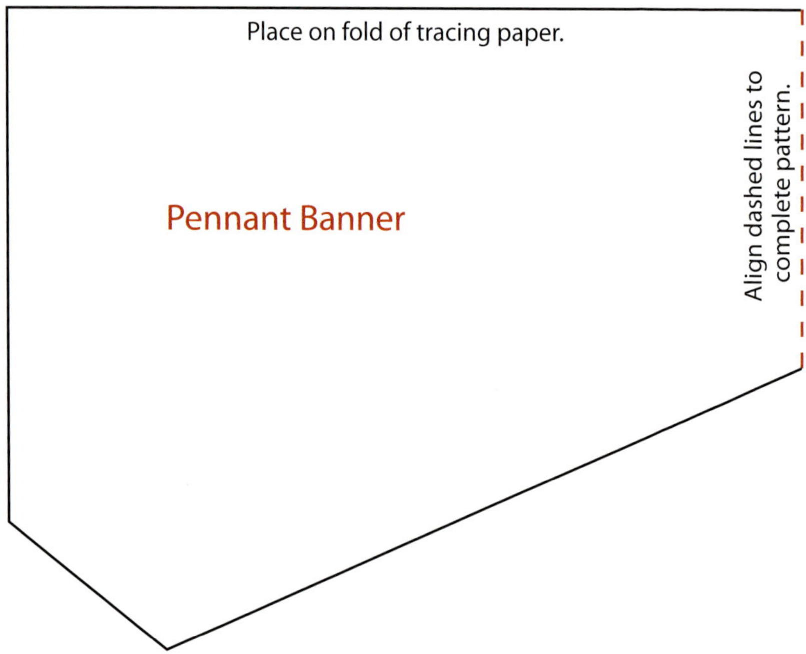
Place on fold of tracing paper.
Pennant Banner
Align dashed lines to complete pattern.

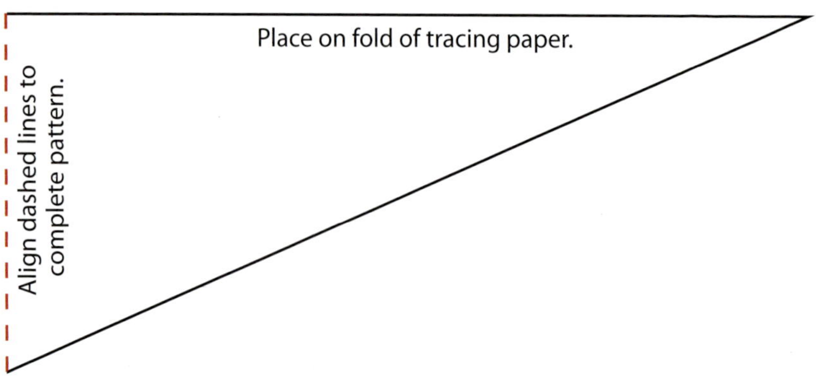
Place on fold of tracing paper.
Align dashed lines to complete pattern.

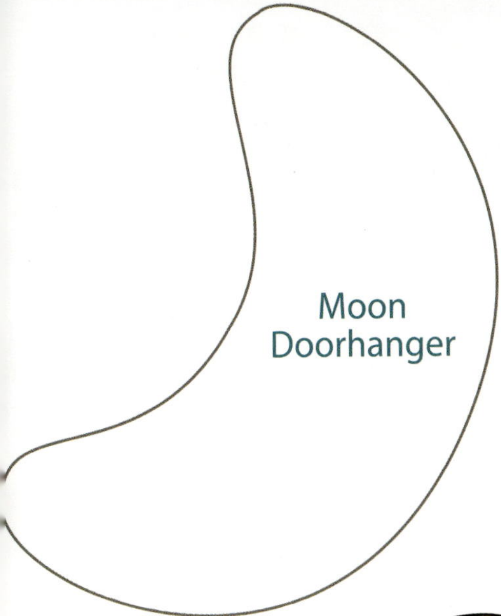
Moon
Doorhanger

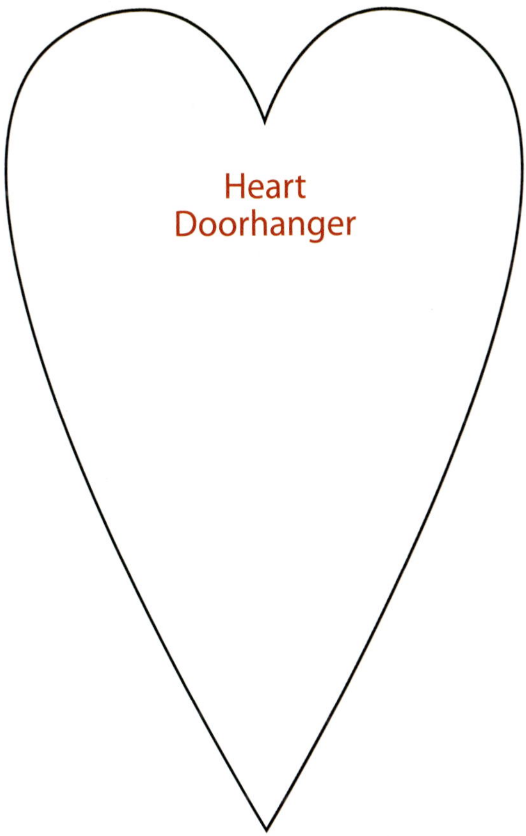
Heart
Doorhanger

meet Holly Witt-Allen

Holly Witt-Allen is in love with creativity. "My style is ever evolving. I like to stay current with trends, learn new techniques, and continually grow as a designer," she says.

"I knew at an early age I would pursue an art career. I graduated with a Bachelor of Fine Arts from Iowa State University and with time found my true passion designing in the craft industry."

She turned to jewelry designing after the frequent moves of her military family made it hard to find a professional job. "Busy with three kids, I began to learn how to make simple beaded earrings. After becoming hooked, I learned how to wire-wrap sea glass, handstamp, solder and fuse metals."

Today, her Witt 'N Whimsy jewelry designs can be seen on Facebook, Pinterest, and www.etsy.com/shop/wittnwhimsy1. Her work is also sold in local shops near her home in a New Jersey seaside community.

Holly's jewelry designs appear in these Leisure Arts books: *Easy Vintage Jewelry* (#6448), *Fanciful Findings* (#6449), *Earthy Boho Jewelry* (#6496), *Beach Chic Jewelry* (#6497), *Jewelry for the Stars* (#6655), and *Bold Unique Jewelry* (#6657).

Production Team: Technical Writer – Mary Sullivan Hutcheson; Editorial Writer – Susan Frantz Wiles; Senior Graphic Artist – Lora Puls; Graphic Artist – Leia Morshedi; Photostylist – Lori Wenger; Photographers – Jason Masters and Ken West.